WATER POLLUTION

Melanie Ostopowich

www.av2books.com

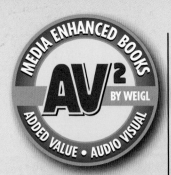

MEDIA ENHANCED BOOKS
AV²
BY WEIGL
ADDED VALUE • AUDIO VISUAL

BOOK CODE

K 8 7 5 8 9 2

AV² by Weigl brings you media enhanced books that support active learning.

AV² provides enriched content that supplements and complements this book. Weigl's AV² books strive to create inspired learning and engage young minds for a total learning experience.

Go to **www.av2books.com**, and enter this book's unique code. You will have access to video, audio, web links, quizzes, a slide show, and activities.

Audio
Listen to sections of the book read aloud.

Video
Watch informative video clips.

Web Link
Find research sites and play interactive games.

Try This!
Complete activities and hands-on experiments.

Due to the dynamic nature of the Internet, some of the URLs and activities provided as part of AV² by Weigl may have changed or ceased to exist. AV² by Weigl accepts no responsibility for any such changes. All media enhanced books are regularly monitored to update addresses and sites in a timely manner. Contact AV² by Weigl at 1-866-649-3445 or av2books@weigl.com with any questions, comments, or feedback.

Published by AV² by Weigl.
350 5th Avenue, 59th Floor
New York, NY 10118
www.av2books.com   www.weigl.com

Library of Congress Cataloging-in-Publication Data

Ostopowich, Melanie.
 Water pollution / Melanie Ostopowich.
     p. cm. -- (Science matters. Water science)
 Includes index.
 ISBN 978-1-61690-004-5 (hardcover : alk. paper) -- ISBN 978-1-61690-010-6 (softcover : alk. paper) -- ISBN 978-1-61690-016-8 (e-book)
 1. Water--Pollution--Juvenile literature. I. Title.
 TD422.O84 2011
 628.1'68078--dc22
                          2009050983

Printed in the United States of America in North Mankato, Minnesota
1 2 3 4 5 6 7 8 9 0 14 13 12 11 10

052010
WEP264000

Project Coordinator Heather C. Hudak
Design Terry Paulhus

Photo Credits
Every reasonable effort has been made to trace ownership and to obtain permission to reprint copyright material. The publishers would be pleased to have any errors or omissions brought to their attention so that they may be corrected in subsequent printings.

Weigl acknowledges Getty Images as its primary image supplier for this title.
World Resources Institute: Pages 12–13 map source.

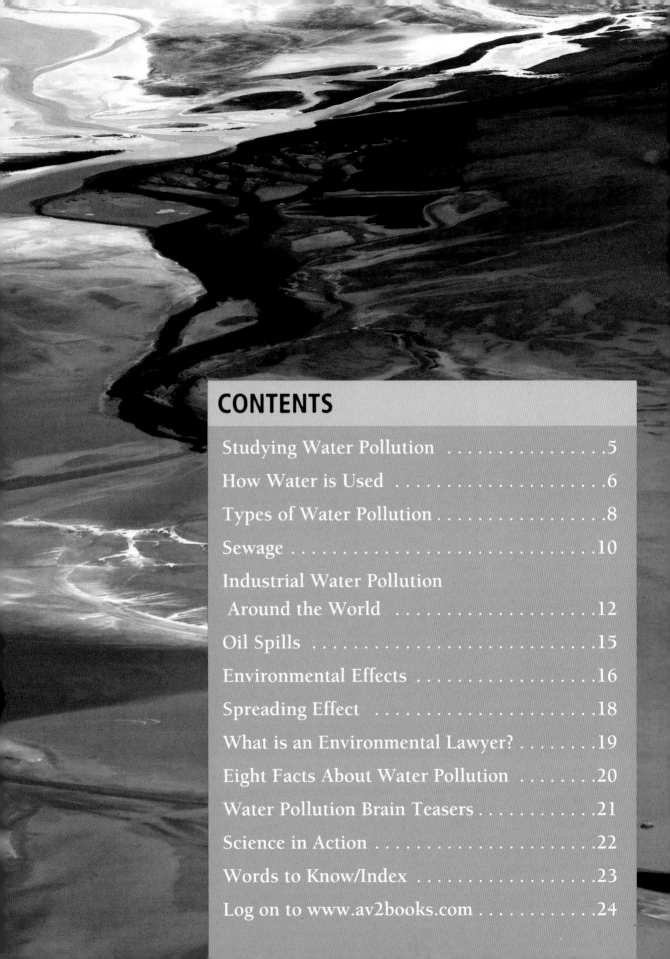

CONTENTS

Rather than using chemicals to help plants grow in home gardens, people can use **compost**. Compost bins are places to put food and garden waste. This waste is broken down by **bacteria**, worms, and other organisms. After it has been broken down, compost can be used to help plants grow. Composting removes the need for harmful chemicals that pollute water.

Studying Water Pollution

Gases, chemicals, and waste can pollute air, water, and soil. Throwing trash into oceans, rivers, and lakes is one way people cause water pollution. The main sources of water pollution are businesses, farming, and **sewage**. Some water pollution can also come from natural sources such as soil. Polluted water can make people and animals ill.

Earth has a limited amount of water. Water **recycles** itself through the **water cycle**. When pollution enters water, it spreads through the water cycle.

One of the main ways water is polluted is if waste is dumped directly into water supplies. Water supplies can become polluted through more indirect channels as well. Emissions from cars and factories can be found in rainwater. Rainwater then travels from the ground into water sources, such as lakes and rivers. To protect water supplies, people need to prevent pollution at all stages of the water cycle.

About 1.2 trillion gallons (4.5 trillion liters) of untreated sewage, stormwater, and industrial waste are poured into the U.S. water system every year.

How Water is Used

People need water. A person can live nearly two months without food, but the same person can live only five to seven days without water.

Water is used for cleaning, heating, and making food. Polluted water can carry diseases. Over long periods of time, people who use polluted water can become ill with diseases such as cancer.

In the United States, a law called the Clean Water Act makes dumping pollutants into water illegal. However, this law is difficult to enforce. Many companies and individuals break this law.

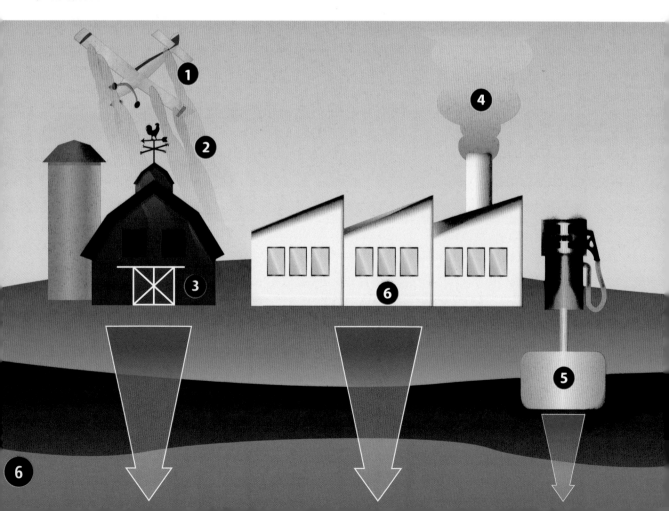

WATER POLLUTION FROM PEOPLE AND COMPANIES

❶ Pesticides
A pesticide is a chemical designed to kill pests, such as insects. Pesticides often are spread by airplanes and can end up in water supplies.

❷ Fertilizers
Farmers use airplanes to spread millions of tons of fertilizers over their land each year. Fertilizers help plants grow, but they can end up in water supplies.

❸ Farming
On farms, animal waste is stored in large lagoons. Lagoons can burst or leak into the ground, which pollutes **groundwater**.

❹ Carbon Monoxide
Carbon monoxide rises from factory and car exhaust pipes into clouds, causing the clouds to become polluted.

❺ Gas Tanks
Leaking gas tanks are common. When they leak, harmful substances seep into the ground and enter water supplies.

❻ Chemical Spills
Chemicals can be toxic, **corrosive**, and even explosive. Chemicals can create fumes, be spilled, or leak. This can lead to chemicals in the water cycle.

❼ Landfills
People dump their garbage in landfills. Water filters through garbage that can contain chemicals or pollutants before seeping into the ground and entering the water cycle.

❽ Chlorine
Chlorine is used to disinfect water supplies and swimming pools. Water used for drinking and bathing often contains small amounts of chlorine.

❾ Pipes
Copper and lead pipes can corrode. As water passes through the pipe, it picks up tiny particles of the metal. This water comes out of the tap polluted.

❿ Acid Rain
Acid rain is a result of pollutants entering the air. Exhaust from cars and factories reacts with water, oxygen, and other harmful chemicals, which creates acid rain.

⓫ Septic Tanks
Some homes store wastewater from kitchens and washrooms underground near the home. Pollution from septic tanks can leak into the ground and enter water supplies.

Types of Water Pollution

Water pollution happens when pollutants end up in bodies of water, either directly or indirectly. Two serious forms of pollution are industrial pollution and agricultural pollution.

Industrial and agricultural pollution are preventable because they are caused by people. This chart outlines different types of water pollution.

NUTRIENT RUNOFF

Nutrient runoff happens when leftover fertilizers and sewage get washed into the sea by rivers. There, they cause plants to grow too much, which robs the water of the oxygen underwater life needs to breathe.

SILTATION

Siltation is when mining, construction, and **dredging** sends dirt, sand, or other materials into river flow. Coastal **ecosystems** may be buried, or the water may become too muddy for underwater life to survive.

TOXIC WASTE

Sewage, industrial waste, and other poisons pollute water and harm underwater life. Some toxins build up in the fat of animals. Others may make underwater animals unable to produce young.

INDUSTRY

Industry creates more than half of the water pollution in the United States. Water is often used to flush away waste, such as unused chemicals and garbage. After water is used, it is called wastewater. Wastewater spreads pollution through oceans, lakes, and rivers.

FARMING

Fertilizers and pesticides used on some farms are often poisonous and **absorbed** into the soil. Chemicals in the soil reach groundwater. Most drinking water comes from groundwater.

OIL

Oil runoff and spills harm marine life, especially in coastal areas.

PLASTICS

Plastic waste can end up in water supplies. A large buildup of plastic containers, old gear, and other debris **endangers** underwater life. Some underwater animals become trapped in debris.

INTRODUCED SPECIES

Introduced species are plants and animals that are moved to a place where they would not normally live. Thousands of underwater animals are moved around the world in the **ballast** water of ships. Introduced species can change the local environment.

Sewage

Human and animal wastes pollute water in the form of sewage. Sewage carries bacteria and disease. People and animals that drink water that has sewage in it can become ill.

Removing litter from storm drains and gutters that lead to lakes and rivers is one way people can help prevent water pollution. Other ways to help prevent water pollution include cleaning up after pets and putting their waste in a garbage can. Pouring chemicals, such as paint, down a drain can be harmful to water supplies. Instead, chemicals can be taken to fire stations to be disposed safely.

In Indonesia, the canals and rivers flood every year and become clogged with garbage. People wade into the flood waters to clean up the garbage.

Water Pollution Timeline

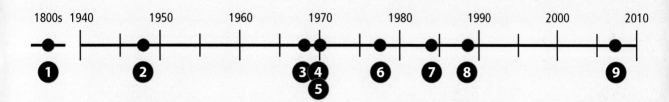

| 1800s | 1940 | 1950 | 1960 | 1970 | 1980 | 1990 | 2000 | 2010 |

1 **2** **3** **4** **5** **6** **7** **8** **9**

1 **Late 18th and early 19th centuries**
The **Industrial Revolution** begins. There is large-scale use of coal for power, which pollutes air and water.

2 **1948**
The U.S. Congress passes the Federal Water Pollution Control Act. This is the first major law to fight water pollution.

3 **1969**
Chemical waste is released into Ohio's Cuyahoga River, causing it to burst into flames.

4 **1970**
The U.S. Environmental Protection Agency (EPA) is established by President Richard Nixon to protect the health of people and the environment. Today, the EPA has about 18,000 employees.

5 **1970**
The first Earth Day is celebrated across the United States. Events highlight the need to protect the nation's natural resources, such as water.

6 **1977**
The Federal Water Pollution Control Act becomes the Clean Water Act. The new law prevents dumping pollution into U.S. waterways.

7 **1984**
In Bhopal, India, thousands of people die, and 120,000 more become seriously ill due to chemicals leaking from a U.S. pesticide plant.

8 **1988**
Needles and other medical waste washes up on New Jersey beaches. Later that year, Congress passes the Ocean Dumping Ban Act, which outlaws dumping certain types of waste into the ocean.

9 **2008**
Human activity causes the ocean to be at its most acidic level in recorded history.

Industrial Water Pollution Around the World

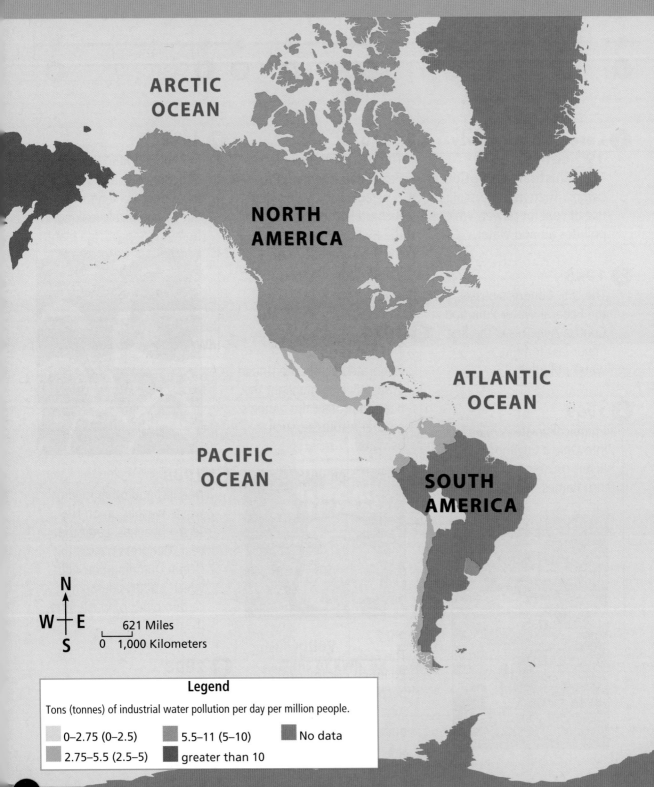

ARCTIC OCEAN

NORTH AMERICA

ATLANTIC OCEAN

PACIFIC OCEAN

SOUTH AMERICA

N
W E
S

621 Miles
0   1,000 Kilometers

Legend

Tons (tonnes) of industrial water pollution per day per million people.

0–2.75 (0–2.5)	5.5–11 (5–10) No data
2.75–5.5 (2.5–5)	greater than 10

WHAT HAVE YOU LEARNED ABOUT INDUSTRIAL WATER POLLUTION?

This map shows industrial water pollution around the world. Use this map, and research online to answer these questions.

1. Which continent produces the most industrial water pollution per day?
2. Which continent produces the least industrial water pollution per day?

ASIA

EUROPE

PACIFIC OCEAN

AFRICA

ATLANTIC OCEAN

INDIAN OCEAN

AUSTRALIA

SOUTHERN OCEAN

ANTARCTICA

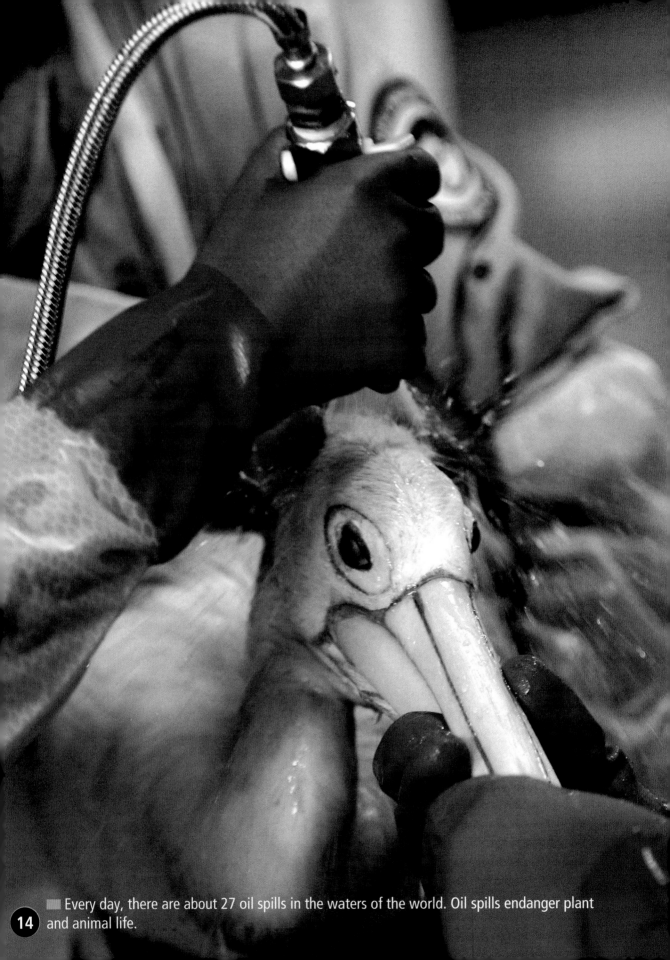

Every day, there are about 27 oil spills in the waters of the world. Oil spills endanger plant and animal life.

Oil Spills

Oil spills in oceans, lakes, and rivers are usually accidental. Oil floats and quickly spreads over the water's surface. A **film** of oil called an oil slick floats on top of the water.

Oil spills are difficult to clean up. Oil coats the feathers of birds, fur of **mammals**, and skin of fish. The animals swallow oil as they try to clean themselves. Oil is poisonous, and the animals often die. Birds are washed with canola oil and dish-washing liquid to remove oil from their feathers.

On March 24, 1989, an oil tanker named the *Exxon Valdez* hit a **reef** near Alaska. The reef tore a hole in the side of the ship. In minutes, oil gushed into the ocean. The ship lost a total of 11 million gallons (41,639,530 L) of oil.

■ More than 1 million gallons (4 million liters) of water can be polluted by 1 gallon (4 L) of oil.

Oil covered and ruined most of the Alaska coast. About 250,000 seabirds, 2,800 sea otters, 300 harbor seals, 250 bald eagles, and 22 whales died. Billions of salmon and herring eggs were also lost when oil swept them into the ocean.

Environmental Effects

Water pollution can come from natural sources. **Landslides** and **erosion** cause loose soil to fall into rivers and lakes. This dumps extra dirt and rock into rivers. Fish have difficulty breathing when there is too much soil in the water.

Water is often used to cool machines in factories. This warms the water. The warmed water is returned to lakes and rivers. This process is called thermal pollution. It causes the amount of oxygen in the water to decrease.

Washing cars in residential driveways is one of the most environmentally damaging chores done at home. Car cleaning products contain harmful pollutants that enter the water supply through storm drains. There are several ways to reduce the damage done from washing a car. One way is for people to wash their cars at commercial car washes. Federal laws require that commercial car washes clean their wastewater before returning it to the water supply. Other ways to be green are to buy environmentally safe car wash products or use less water to rinse the vehicle.

Animals need water to live, just as people do. Animals living in polluted water can become ill quickly.

Many animals, such as whales and seals, make their homes in water. For example, fish breathe oxygen from water. Water plants also rely on clean water for oxygen. Polluted water loses some of its oxygen. Fish and plants cannot live without the oxygen in water.

▨ Ash and smoke from volcanic eruptions rise into the air and can create acid rain. Acid rain enters water supplies, affecting plant and animal life.

Spreading Effect

Water is always moving. Bodies of water move along paths called currents. Tides are the regular rise and fall of the water level in the ocean.

The change in water level is caused by the pull of the Sun and Moon on Earth. When pollution enters water, the pollution moves with the currents and tides. Pollution does not stay in one place.

Land-based pollutants, such as garbage and sewage, make up about 44 percent of all pollution entering Earth's oceans.

What is an Environmental Lawyer?

A environmental lawyer is someone who creates and enforces laws dealing with the environment. They work in the areas of **conservation**, **stewardship**, and reducing pollution.

Robert F. Kennedy, Jr.

Robert F. Kennedy, Jr. is an environmental lawyer. He is well-known for his work to protect the environment. Kennedy belongs to the Waterkeeper Alliance and Riverkeeper. Both groups work to keep water clean and unpolluted.

Working Conditions

Environmental lawyers spend a great deal of time studying environmental laws. They often act as advisors and take part in court cases.

Tools

Environmental lawyers use legal books to do research and build cases. They must have strong reason and debate skills to win cases.

Eight Facts About Water Pollution

The Great Lakes supply water to one out of every seven people in the United States. More than 360 dangerous chemicals have been found in the Great Lakes.

More than 5 million people die each year from diseases caused by unsafe drinking water. Eighty percent are children under five years of age.

Plastic waste in coastal areas can kill more than 100,000 mammals and 1 million seabirds each year.

Around the British coastline, 331 million tons (300 million tonnes) of sewage flow into the sea every day.

About 80 percent of the pollution in seas and oceans comes from land-based activities.

More than 1 billion people in the world do not have access to safe water.

In one week, the people on a cruise ship can create enough human sewage to fill 10 backyard swimming pools.

About 40 percent of rivers in the United States are too polluted for fishing, swimming, and other aquatic sports.

Water Pollution
Brain Teasers

1 What is wastewater?

2 How many people die each year from drinking unsafe water?

3 What is the name of the oil tanker that spilled oil in the ocean in 1989?

4 Who is Robert F. Kennedy, Jr.?

5 Does oil sink or float in water?

6 How long can a person live without water?

7 What is thermal pollution?

8 What happens when pollution enters a lake?

9 How does water pollution harm fish and plants?

10 Why is an oil spill dangerous to animals?

Effects of an Oil Spill

You can create an oil spill at home to see how oil pollution affects water.

Tools Needed

food coloring   cooking oil   clear bowl   water

large spoon   small bowl   cleaning supplies, such as paper towels, napkins, and a sponge

Directions

1 In the small bowl, mix some cooking oil with food coloring.

2 Fill the clear bowl halfway with water.

3 Carefully, add one or two spoonfuls of the cooking oil and food coloring mixture to the clear bowl of water. Do not stir the oil into the water. What happens?

4 Now, try to remove the oil from the water using your cleaning supplies. How easy is it to remove the oil from the bowl of water? Imagine if this was an oil spill in the ocean. What would happen to the animals and fish that live there?

Words to Know

absorbed: soaked up

bacteria: one-celled organisms

ballast: heavy material that is used to keep a ship stable

compost: a mixture of decaying plant matter that is used as fertilizer

conservation: the careful use of a resource so that it lasts longer

corrosive: a substance that eats away at objects

dredging: removing sand, silt, dirt, or other materials from the bottom of a river

ecosystems: communities of living things sharing an environment

endangers: puts animals at risk of harm

erosion: the removal of rock and pieces of soil by natural forces such as running water, ice, waves, and wind

film: a thin layer or covering

groundwater: water beneath Earth's surface

Industrial Revolution: a time of great progress with the creation of many factories

landslides: rocks and soil that slide down a slope

mammals: animals that have hair, are warm-blooded, and feed their young with milk

recycles: returns to an original condition so a process can begin again

reef: a chain of rocks or ridge of sand at or near the surface of water

sewage: waste from sinks, toilets, and other devices in homes and factories

stewardship: to take care of the environment

water cycle: the process of water disappearing into the sky and returning to the ground

Index

23

Log on to www.av2books.com

AV[2] by Weigl brings you media enhanced books that support active learning. Go to **www.av2books.com**, and enter the special code inside the front cover of this book. You will gain access to enriched and enhanced content that supplements and complements this book. Content includes video, audio, web links, quizzes, a slide show, and activities.

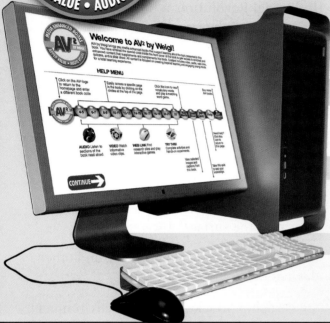

Audio
Listen to sections of the book read aloud.

Video
Watch informative video clips.

Web Link
Find research sites and play interactive games.

Try This!
Complete activities and hands-on experiments.

WHAT'S ONLINE?

Try This! Complete activities and hands-on experiments.	**Web Link** Find research sites and play interactive games.	**Video** Watch informative video clips.	**EXTRA FEATURES**
Pages 6-7 Try this activity about water pollution from people and companies	**Pages 6-7** Find out more about how people use water	**Pages 4-5** Watch a video about water pollution	**Audio** Hear introductory audio at the top of every page.
Pages 10-11 Use this timeline activity to test your knowledge of world events	**Pages 16-17** Link to more information about how water pollution affects the environment	**Pages 8-9** Check out a video about the effects of water pollution	**Key Words** Study vocabulary, and play a matching word game.
Pages 12-13 Use this map to learn about industrial water pollution around the world	**Pages 18-19** Learn more about being an environmental lawyer	**Pages 14-15** View how oil spills affect the environment	**Slide Show** View images and captions, and try a writing activity.
Pages 18-19 Write about a day in the life of an environmental lawyer	**Page 20** Link to facts about water pollution		**AV[2] Quiz** Take this quiz to test your knowledge
Page 22 Try the activity in the book, then play an interactive game			

Due to the dynamic nature of the Internet, some of the URLs and activities provided as part of AV[2] by Weigl may have changed or ceased to exist. AV[2] by Weigl accepts no responsibility for any such changes. All media enhanced books are regularly monitored to update addresses and sites in a timely manner. Contact AV[2] by Weigl at 1-866-649-3445 or av2books@weigl.com with any questions, comments, or feedback.